Bill Byars is a Christian gentleman as well as a counselor and author. His new book will be a blessing to those who are considering a second marriage. He deals with the emotional recovery of divorce, how to find God's purpose for our lives and how to choose a potential mate in marriage for the second time around. What a "timely book" for those who want to heal and move forward from a broken first marriage.

Dr. Greg Mathis, Senior Pastor,
Mud Creek Baptist Church

Bill Byars, with clear words and the heart of his personal and professional experience, coaches those considering marriage for a second time. If you are divorced and considering re-marriage, you will be well-served to consider the guidance and instruction provided in these pages.

Dr. Donna Gibbs
Director, *A Clear Word* Counseling Center

MARRIAGE THE
SECOND
TIME AROUND

W.R. BYARS

MARRIAGE THE SECOND TIME AROUND

Or Getting it Right the First Time

TATE PUBLISHING
AND ENTERPRISES, LLC

The author invites comments, suggestions,
and testimonies (with permission to
print) to blbyars@hotmail.com.

This book is designed to provide accurate and authoritative information with regard to the subject matter covered. This information is given with the understanding that neither the author nor Tate Publishing, LLC is engaged in rendering legal, professional advice. Since the details of your situation are fact dependent, you should additionally seek the services of a competent professional.

The opinions expressed by the author are not necessarily those of Tate Publishing, LLC.

Published by Tate Publishing & Enterprises, LLC
127 E. Trade Center Terrace | Mustang, Oklahoma 73064 USA
1.888.361.9473 | www.tatepublishing.com

Tate Publishing is committed to excellence in the publishing industry. The company reflects the philosophy established by the founders, based on Psalm 68:11,

"The Lord gave the word and great was the company of those who published it."

Book design copyright © 2012 by Tate Publishing, LLC. All rights reserved.
Cover design by Kristen Verser
Interior design by Lynly D. Grider
Author photo by Kathy Glover
Figure illustrations by Mark Lucas

Published in the United States of America

ISBN: 978-1-61862-148-1
1. Religion / Christian Life / Love & Marriage
2. Religion / Christian Ministry / Counseling & Recovery
11.12.12

DEDICATION

This book is prayerfully dedicated to my Lord and Savior, Jesus Christ, for the privilege of sharing life's experiences with others; to my wife, Lynn, for sharing the reward of joy in helping to restore hope in the hearts, souls and minds of others; to the hundreds who have rewarded our tears with changed lives to the glory of the Father, Son, and Holy Spirit. Amen.

ACKNOWLEDGMENTS

Without God's providence, this book would not have been written. Without my wife Lynn's encouragement and willingness to sacrifice some of our time together, this book would not have been written.

To the many others who have contributed knowingly or unknowingly, I give my heartfelt gratitude to each. To name a few: Ron Wiebe, Dr. Dean Smith, Dr. Mark Lauterbach, Dave Grayson, Dr. Mark Platt, Randy Romeo, Dr. Ralph Kraft and the 1976-2003 staff of the First Baptist Church of Los Altos, California, the present staff at Mud Creek Baptist Church (Hendersonville, North Carolina), and its senior pastor, Dr. Greg Mathis, as well as Dr. Donna Gibbs and her staff at the Clear Word Counseling Center in Hendersonville, North Carolina.

Just as important, if not more so, are the hundreds that I have been privileged to counsel as a pastor and Bible coach. Among these, along with my wife Lynn, are the many that attended our Friday night Divorce Recovery Group, the DRG, in California and the couples attending the premarital classes in North Carolina. I have learned so much from them. May God richly bless each one of you.

Without the staff at Tate Publishing, you would be looking at a ream of blank pages. Thank you, Tate! In particular, I wish to thank Thomas Beard, my editor at Tate, for his encouragement and wise counsel.

My thanks also to Herbert Morris and Mary Cervini. They each contributed their time and experience to educate me in the computer art of "color editing".

TABLE OF CONTENTS

FOREWORD

There are six parts to this book. My wife, Lynn, and I have personally lived through each one of them. If the sharing of our experiences and of the source of our strength will benefit just one family it will have been a labor well worth doing.

It is our belief that before a second marriage (with or without children) can begin, the *baggage* from the past must be dealt with. Forgiveness must be given and accepted. This is an imperative. To forgive is a decision of the will, not the emotions. Do not let emotions lead you astray. There will come a time in your singleness, a point of acceptance, where if you meet someone suitable for marriage, great! And if you don't, life is still great!

To help arrive at forgiveness and the point of acceptance, this book has been divided up into six parts as follows:

Part one, "Recovery," deals with the emotional trauma associated with going through a divorce, recognizing the grief cycle, and coming to terms with it by giving and accepting forgiveness for yourself and for your ex-spouse.

Part two, "God's Way," discusses how to find faith and hope by appropriating the power available from the Creator of life.

Part three, "Victory," is about how to live life to the fullest in mind, body, and spirit as a single with or without children.

Part four, "The Courtship," is about having freedom in dealing with the opposite sex in a non-threatening way, a way to discover more about the character and personality of a possible friend for life.

Part five, "Is This the One for Me?" discusses how to avoid the mistakes of the past to insure the success of a future marital relationship, together with learning new skills and methods of communicating, problem-solving, and planning.

Part six, "Blending Two Families into One," deals with identifying the obstacles to be faced, the necessity for parents to demonstrate a united parental front to their children, how to show love and affection to each of the children in a way that builds acceptance and trust between all family members, and the need to be firm, fair, and consistent in all family relationships.

Over the past thirty years, I have gained the experience to articulate all this while working as a pastoral counselor (California) and Bible coach (North Carolina), and while leading, with my wife, the premarital course in NC, as well as an ongoing Friday night Divorce Recovery Group (DRG) in our California home. The DRG lasted over fourteen years and has been our most fulfilling ministry in our service for the Lord. May each reader of this book share in the blessings we have received.

One final note: although many of the examples and anecdotes in this book are based on true events, the details and the names of the parties involved have been changed to protect their confidentiality.

PART ONE:

RECOVERY

THE FIRST MARRIAGE: WHAT WENT WRONG?

Are you contemplating a second marriage? Have you healed from the trauma of divorce from your first marriage? The experts claim that it takes one year for every four years of marriage to attain the state of acceptance (ready to move forward in your new life as a single with or without children). From sources quoted in the www.divorce.org and the Center for Disease Control's Divorce Statistics Manual, it is stated that twenty to forty percent of all second marriages end in divorce within the first ten years. Now that is scary! It is even more frightening if the second marriage takes place within two years from the date of the divorce. That divorce rate is seventy to eighty percent. Marrying in haste for any of the following reasons certainly isn't the answer:

- "I'm lonely." Usually, this is a reason given by women.
- "I need sex." Usually, this is a reason given by men.
- "My children need a father or (mother)." Whoever is the primary keeper of the children will usually

voice this as a reason. It is a valid reason but not as an excuse for marrying in haste.

- "Security." Usually a reason given by women. This rates high on a woman's priority list, as well it should, but not as an excuse for marriage.
- "I want to be part of a couple." (It's a couples' world.) A toss-up, with the edge to the ladies.
- "Financial needs." This, in my view, tops the list as a major reason why women, in particular, marry for the wrong reason. Too many men renege on their responsibility to pay child support and/or alimony, leaving women, in some cases, destitute. The resulting marriage becomes a "marriage of convenience," not one of true affection. In all likelihood this marriage, too, will fail.
- Other. (What would you add?)

_____

_____

_____

_____

In most of the examples above, the woman is the most vulnerable and therefore the most likely to enter into a relationship that will be susceptible to failure, whether it is a live-in arrangement or a marriage. Do not let emotions such as fear or anxiety control your decision-making. There are answers to this terrible situation. That is why you are reading this book. Be patient and read it through. Write in your comments and thoughts in the spaces provided. Share them with someone you trust.

First, what can be done to increase the chances for a successful second marriage? Start with understanding why the first marriage failed. It is most important that you not only understand why, but that you have come to terms with the issues involved to the point, and this is key, of not only having forgiven yourself but the other party as well. This next exercise will help you arrive at that stage of healing if you haven't already.

NINE CAUSES FOR DIVORCE

This section may be very painful as you reflect on the past. You may resurrect some past memories that have been buried deep within your psyche because of the anguish that they caused. So be aware this may happen.

Now, realistically appraise the causes that led to the divorce. Were any of the following a contributing factor to the destruction of the marriage, and if so, what was your share of the blame? Using a pencil, elaborate on each of the following factors:

ADULTERY: Even if it only happened once, is a deep betrayal of the other spouse. Trust, like a brand new rubber band, once stretched, never returns to its original shape. Suspicion will rear its ugly head at every unexplained phone call, text message, or absence. Perhaps that's one of the reasons why the Bible permits divorce for the sin of adultery. Yet the Bible also says to forgive seventy times seven. Suspicion and anger will diminish over time and wounds will heal, but it takes a dedicated effort by both husband and wife to make it happen. That was included as part of the marriage vows, right?

Incredible as it may seem, the bride, while on the honeymoon cruise to the Hawaiian Islands slept with an officer of the ship's crew not once but several times. Needless to say the marriage was over before the cruise ship made port. She is still in therapy. Did something similar happen to you?

_____

_____

_____

_____

A CAREER: How many executives, building a career, have neglected their spouse and children with the alibi "I'm doing it for us"? Long hours, work on the weekends, travel overnight or for long periods of time only exacerbate the problem. Yet, conversely, this can become an excuse for the abandoned spouse to seek comfort with someone else "…because I'm lonely." Or the lonely partner may seek employment or activities of their own, leading to further separation. "We just grew apart."

It was not uncommon during the boom years in California's "Silicon Valley" for the husband to bring into his place of employment a cot for rest during the 24-to-36-or-more-hour spurts of activity required to bring an innovative product to market. The monetary rewards, when a company went public, were astronomical. It was said that during this time 25 new millionaires came into being each day. But at what cost to the home? And that doesn't count the thousands who also sacrificed much without catching the brass ring as the "merry-go-round" turned. They lost doubly. But good divorce lawyers were in high demand. They commanded fees in excess of $500 per hour plus expenses. And this was 30 to 40 years ago. I can't help but wonder what these fees are today.

What can you add about this tragedy?

_____

_____

_____

_____

IN-LAWS: Sometimes mother-in-law jokes are not very funny; they hit too close to home. So, too, are some father-in-law jokes. While I personally have never witnessed a divorce solely on the grounds of "interfering in-laws," there is no doubt in my mind and experience that they can be a contributing factor.

Too often a well intentioned in-law will volunteer advice on how to rear children or how to handle other domestic problems. Usually the advice is offered to their son or daughter, as the case may be, causing friction between the husband and wife, as well as between the in-laws. One such case ended with the wife telling the in-law, in no uncertain terms, to "buzz off". The husband had failed to support his wife. That became one of the reasons that lead to divorce.

In my view, there were two instances in this case that were not handled correctly. The husband should have been the one to confront his parents, not the wife; and secondly the in-laws should not have offered advice unless it was asked for by the couple.

ABUSE, PHYSICAL: Abuse usually targets the wife and/ or the children. Hopefully, you removed yourself from such a scene to a sanctuary of some sort and the abuser was either incarcerated, given psychological therapy, or both. In either case, the woman and her children will, in all likelihood, need counseling to help heal the damage caused, in particular, by the words of abuse. Lest we think that it is all one way, there is many a woman who has "flayed" her husband's or child's ego with an acid tongue. That also is a two-way street.

One marriage ended when the wife, a woman of substantial proportions, threw her husband down the stairs when he arrived home under the influence of alcohol. It turned out that this was not the first time he had been so punished for his over-indulgence, but it was the last. He sued for divorce as soon as he was released from the hospital. She was fortunate that he didn't have her charged with assault. Sorry to say it didn't end his addiction to alcohol.

Did abuse play a part in the destruction of your marriage? How has it affected your attitude toward the opposite sex?

_____

_____

_____

_____

Do you still feel fear, anxiety, and anger?

_____

_____

_____

ADDICTIONS: To alcohol, drugs, gambling, and pornography: the victim here is a slave to their habit(s), with the result that the habit is a higher priority than the spouse. The habit becomes all-encompassing. Only a person who has gone through the agony and despair of watching a loved one fall prey to such an addiction can truly understand it, if even then. It is even worse if you were the one with the habit.

The efforts of one set of divorced parents to rescue their teenage son, a handsome boy of promise, from the ravages caused by drugs were all for naught when he died of an overdose. Was he, like so many others caught in the web of addiction, a victim of a broken family? While the divorce of his parents no doubt influenced his life, he made a conscious decision to do drugs. He paid the consequences for his choice. Hopefully the parents, in their grief, have come to this understanding.

What is your story?

FINANCES: Usually, the problem with finances is the ubiquitous credit card. Was it far too easy to allow the credit card to become the "master" of the house? Spending beyond one's means has brought down many a marriage.

One couple, using five credit cards, ran up a total debt of well over $50,000. They had to file for bankruptcy, destroying their credit worthiness and their marriage. The sad part of this story was that the husband was self-employed as a financial planner.

Was this ever a source of a heated argument in your house? Do you live on a budget now? Do you have credit cards now? How many?

_____

_____

_____

_____

_____

_____

FAILURE TO COMMUNICATE: Communication is more than just words. It includes a touch, a smile, a written word or doing something for the other person that is out of the ordinary. Problems cannot be worked out or solved if communication fails. Each party has to be completely honest in setting forth their position and not just listen, but hear what the other person is saying.

A serious failure to communicate was exemplified by one husband who would come home from work, eat dinner, then remove himself to his computer. He would spend the rest of the evening engrossed in the screen, much to the dismay of his wife. She felt abandoned and unloved. She suspected that he may also have been involved in pornography. If so, it was a double failure on the part of the husband.

Was failure to communicate part of the problem?
How?

_____

_____

_____

_____

DISCIPLINING OF CHILDREN: Was there too much discipline, not enough, or was it somewhere in the middle? Was discipline applied fairly, firmly, and consistently? Did the children fear one parent more than the other? Did they fear both?

One father, on coming home from a lengthy business trip, would ask the mother if their son had misbehaved during the father's absence. The answer was always yes; whether this was warranted or not, I don't know. Nevertheless, the son always received a severe beating at the homecoming. The son came to expect it. Today there is no contact between them. The son's four children have no idea that they have another set of grandparents. No one has won in this situation, not even the innocent grandchildren. They have lost, too. What are your thoughts on discipline or lack thereof?

_____

_____

_____

_____

Other, you name it. This is a catchall category. Whatever else it was that contributed to the breakup, put it here. Desertion? Prison? The "glow" is gone?

_____

_____

_____

_____

_____

_____

Finished? Are you certain?

You may very well be asking at this juncture, *Why am I doing this exercise? All it does is bring up unhappy memories.* But that is the point. Each contributing factor, listed above, needs to be evaluated and your share of the responsibility accepted. Forgive yourself and ask your ex-mate to forgive you as you forgive them. Hard to do, isn't it? Even if it needs to be done it may still be too painful, but that is your choice. Nevertheless, it still needs to be done at some point in time. More will be said later in the next chapter on how to climb this mountain. But before we move on, take as long as necessary to meditate (do it out loud) on what *you* could have done differently to mitigate each of the contributing factors. Use the following space to write (in pencil) your response.

_____

_____

Done? No doubt your ex-spouse would need a ream of paper to confess their share of the guilt. Right? Wait twenty-four hours. Then go back over what you have written down. Read it aloud. Listen to the tone of your voice. What did you hear? Use the eraser on that pencil to correct, change, or add to what you have written. Do this every so often as you go through the healing process.

It is critical, in my view, that you recognize and come to terms with the reality, the truth, of what behavior or actions, by either party, brought about the destruction of the marriage. The foregoing exercises are meant to do just that. The next chapter will show you how to identify and handle the emotions that these actions have aroused within you.

NOTES:

_____

_____

_____

_____

_____

_____

_____

_____

_____

_____

_____

_____

_____

_____

_____

_____

_____

_____

_____

ON THE WAY TO RECOVERY

I t is important to understand the grief cycle associated with divorce. Elizabeth Kübler-Ross in her book on *Death and Dying* propounded a theory that involved a series of emotional states that have been referred to as the "grief cycle." This cycle is the same for the death of a relationship as it is for the death of a person with one exception—closure. With divorce, the other party is still around, and where children are involved, the pain of divorce will reoccur in varying degrees as you come in contact with your ex-mate at school events, graduations, weddings, birth of grandchildren, etc., and for some, when the former spouse marries again and your children are participating in the wedding ceremony. The pain becomes almost unbearable.

It is imperative, from my experience, that this grief cycle be understood and the emotions that it evokes are faced and dealt with in order to reach acceptance and ultimately forgiveness as soon as possible. Remember, one year for every four years of marriage, or marry too soon and in all likelihood be back in the divorce courts in less than two years.

The grief cycle theory as defined by Kübler-Ross consists of five emotional states: denial, anger, bargaining, depression, and acceptance. These stages will alternate throughout the recovery. For divorce, I would add a final step: forgiveness.

In the many years that my wife and I led a weekly divorce recovery program, we have witnessed the empirical validity of Kübler-Ross' proposed theory, even more so when the act of forgiveness is given and granted.

Starting with *denial,* the partner initiating the divorce has already plotted out the steps required to bring about the severance of the marriage. The other partner, in most cases, is caught off guard and just can't believe that a divorce is imminent or in process. The Friday night group came up with names for each person in the process. However indelicate as it sounds, it usually evoked laughter: the "dumper" and the "dumpee".

Anger soon follows denial, anger strong enough for one woman to seek out a pawn shop to buy a gun. Fortunately for her, her husband, and his paramour, the shops were closed in deference to Yom Kipper and St. Patrick's Day. Why? It was an agreement between the Irish and the Jews to honor each other's holiday by both closing shop on those days. That twenty-four hour delay was long enough for reason to prevail.

Another woman, in revenge, dragged her husband's undershorts through a patch of poison ivy before he had the opportunity to "rescue" all of his belongings from his former abode. Upon hearing this story, everyone enjoyed a deep belly laugh at the envisioned discomfort of the dumper when the rash and itching started. The husband couldn't help but wonder whether he'd somehow picked up an STD. "Where did I get it? And from whom?"

A third woman, when her ex-spouse-to-be came to collect his belongings, threw everything out of the second-story window, including his TV. It didn't survive. Neither did the marriage.

Bargaining is usually the next step before depression. Unfortunately, bargaining taking the form of "I'll change, don't leave me" rarely works. It is usually one-sided, and if a third party is involved, no amount of change by just the "dumpee" will bring about a restoration of the marital relationship.

With no hope for reconciliation, *depression* sets in if it hasn't already. Depression is a terrible state of mind for those in it as well as for those who care about the person suffering through it. It is not only debilitating mentally and physically but spiritually as well.

By working through the grief cycle process, *acceptance* can finally be reached. This may take months and even years and sadly for some, never. Like deer caught in the headlights of an oncoming car, they become immobile, frozen in place. For relief, some seek help from the medical profession, usually ending up on medication, but others seek support from self-help groups as well as from the clergy. These can be helpful. But it has been my experience that only a relationship with our Creator will eventually bring about acceptance and the ability to forgive the departed spouse as well as yourself.

The final healing step for divorce is forgiveness. It is not necessary for your well being that your apology be accepted – but the fact that you have sincerely asked for forgiveness and simultaneously granted forgiveness to the ex-spouse releases you from feelings of guilt. If the ex-spouse refuses to grant forgiveness when you ask for it, it becomes their problem, not yours. There is nothing more that you can do, except practice civility. It is amazing how your stress level drops, and you feel the joy and peace of release.

You may well ask what is forgiveness and how do I forgive? The perfect example of forgiveness is given by God, the Father. He doesn't remember sins. They have been erased by the Cross (more on this in the next chapter). But we, as imperfect human beings, do remember. They are like scars. Every so often the scar is torn open for one reason or another. We remember and emotions surface. It takes an act of the will to overcome the emotions and seal, once again, the scar. Don't be discouraged. It takes time and practice to do this. You will prevail.

In my reading, I have concluded that marriage is between two human beings who have become one flesh and separation, divorce, is a tearing of that flesh. It hurts just as if it were literally flesh. We are spiritual beings, and as such, only the presence of God in this process of healing can true healing (forgiveness) be brought about. The next chapter explains how to find that relationship with God through His Son, Jesus Christ.

PART TWO:

GOD'S WAY

BUILDING ON A NEW FOUNDATION

Do you realize that the reading of these words is indicative of a divine appointment with God? He is calling you to establish a relationship with Him through His Son, Jesus Christ. He wants you to be empowered through the work of the Holy Spirit to begin a new life, one filled with love, joy, peace, patience, and other blessings. This does not mean that you will be free of trials and troubles. Indeed, you may encounter even more. But you will now have the power within you to cope with them.

Now if you decide that this isn't true, that this is a bunch of nonsense or just plain foolishness, skip this chapter and go on to the next. Prior to this time, you have basically trusted in man. Why not try trusting in the Creator of the Universe and his Son Jesus? It is simple to do. Just acknowledge that Jesus is who He says He is, God Incarnate and accept Him as your Savior.

God's truth is still applicable whether you believe in Him or not. His Word is just like the rain. It falls on both the believer and nonbeliever as well, so that both benefit. This is called common grace.

If you are a believer, you too can skip this chapter. However, you may find it worthwhile to read the following and, if necessary, recommit yourself to the lordship of Jesus Christ, your Savior.

Where do you begin as a nonbeliever? Start with acknowledging the truth that God exists, that He created the universe, that He created man in His image all for His good pleasure. There are people of all persuasions who deny these facts with ridicule and theories, e.g. the cosmos always existed ("What about the Big Bang and intelligent design?"), that man evolved from a single cell ("Where did it come from?"), that there is no God.

What nonsense! What utter foolishness! God has revealed Himself through His very creation. Stand on a mountaintop or seashore and view the heavens, the Milky Way, the sunrise and the moonrise and their setting, the beauty of nature everywhere, the seasons and even the storms; witness the miracle of birth and then try and tell yourself that it is all happenstance. The detractors who do so deny God because, I believe, to admit that He exists would reveal that they stand guilty and condemned before Him, just as we all do. It is pride. It is pride in the humanistic belief, as intimated by Abraham Maslow's theory, the "Hierarchy Of Needs," that by attaining the final plateau of self-actualization, we will be like gods. I have never met anyone who even remotely resembles someone who has attained "self-actualization." Have you?

God has further revealed Himself through the written word, the Bible. The prophets, writing under the inspiration of the Holy Spirit, describe God's character, His truth, righteousness, His love for us, and His plan to redeem us through the work and sacrifice of His Son, Jesus Christ. Read what God has to say about Himself in Psalm 119.

Jesus, without sin, took our sins, past, present, and future, upon Himself on the cross of Calvary. We deserve to be punished for our sins, yet He paid our debt, presenting us as righteous to God the Father. Jesus was crucified, buried, and arose alive from the grave on the third day and is now seated with the Father. That is the gospel message. Read further on what the gospel of John has to say about the divinity of Christ. Are you satisfied that Jesus is who He says He is, God Incarnate? If so, are you ready to accept Him as your Savior, your Redeemer, and Counselor and surrender yourself, mind, body, and soul to His Lordship?

A testimony: WB and LJ (North Carolina) had both been divorced, had met, and were in love. Marriage was imminent. But the question that kept nagging at both their consciences was, "Why will this marriage be any different from our first marriages?" Neither one wanted to go through the agony and pain of divorce again. In fact, both had concluded that it would be better to live apart as singles and go their separate ways than in a marital relationship that could flounder and most likely, once again, end up in the divorce courts. They found the answer. It began with a relationship with Jesus Christ as their Savior. That was over thirty-four years ago. They are still happily married.

A testimony from CK (California): "After a physically and emotionally abusive first marriage that ended in divorce, I went through many years of distancing myself from the Lord and at the same time yearning to be married again. This led to relationships that were not healthy, but in my rebellion, I continued to pursue them.

"The Lord gradually softened my heart, and this led me to attend a seminar put on by my pastor, wherein he described the joy of a Christian marriage with both participants completely dedicated to the Lord.

"After that eye-opening experience, I realized that I would never be happy in a marriage if the Lord were not in the center of it. From that came the resolve that I would not remarry unless it were to a man who was completely sold out to his relationship with God.

"So with this resolve being made, which was a huge decision for me, I so wanted to be married again, but that meant waiting upon the Lord. Just a few months later, God brought into my life such a man. Now almost thirty wonderful years later, I still look back in amazement at how much greater God's plan is for our lives than our own plans. But first He had to get my attention and obedience."

A testimony from YEC (California): "When I was a little girl, I remember negotiating with the Almighty. 'Dear God,' I'd pray, 'I promise to be a good girl for the rest of my life if you grant me this one wish.' Although those prayers were never answered, I never gave up bartering all throughout middle school, high school, and college. I found myself continuing to barter with God with everything from getting married and taking care of my children to supporting myself when my husband left me and our two children. I envisioned God to be a go-to person when I had a need, all the while expecting Him to answer my urgent and desperate prayers, like a knight in shining armor riding to rescue me. With my prayers unanswered, I began to doubt God's existence and His love and care for me. Eight years later, still not having God in my life, I made the decision to marry again a man of my own choosing. We created a son who continues to bring me tremendous joy. This marriage also ended in divorce. I finally humbled myself and cried out to God to untangle the mess I had made of my life. Ever since that day, I have exchanged bartering to seeking His will in every aspect of my life.

"I've even come to be thankful for the trials I've experienced. I know that through them, God has made into the person I am today, a new and hopefully improved version, full of much more grace and love. Just when I was happy and contented with my new found life in Christ alone, He lifted the fog, and the sun shone again when He brought to me a wonderful 'God-fearing' man for a husband."

In each of the three foregoing testimonies, there is a common thread, a foundation upon which these marriages were built. The following diagram, Figure 1, God's Design, shows the relationships that exist between the five participants: God the Father, Jesus Christ the Son, the Holy Spirit, the husband, and the wife. The first priority for each, husband and wife, is God through His Son, Jesus Christ. The second priority for the husband is his wife; conversely, the wife's second priority is her husband. Last of all is self, as exemplified by Jesus sacrificing Himself on the cross for each of us. More will be said about priorities in a later chapter. Note that the

Holy Spirit binds everyone together. He is our counselor and our teacher. This is why the Bible instructs us not to become unequally yoked with a nonbeliever.

FIGURE 1 | GOD'S DESIGN

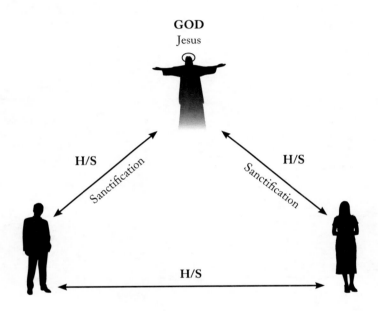

- H&W joined together by the H/S (equally yoked)
- H/S joins H&W to Jesus (God)
- H&W each have equal status with Jesus
- Overseeing the relationship is God the Father. Picture that as an umbrella of protection covering the triangular relationship.
- The closer H&W draw to Christ (through progressive sanctification) the closer they grow to one another.

My prayer for you at this moment is that you have been encouraged by the foregoing three testimonies enough so that you have made the commitment to Jesus. If you did, you now have the power and wisdom of Jesus through the Holy Spirit to meet all of life's challenges. In the next chapter you will begin to feel victory as you apply, in your life, the suggestions presented.

PART THREE:

VICTORY

VICTORY AS A SINGLE

Before contemplating a second trip to the altar, have you reached the state of acceptance and forgiveness regarding the first marriage? Do you understand and acknowledge your contribution to the failure of that marriage? Have you truly forgiven yourself as well as your former spouse? If so, then the first two steps in healing and strengthening the possibility for a successful second marriage have been taken.

The third step involves the understanding of what it means to reach a "point of acceptance" when, in your new life of acceptance and forgiveness, it becomes clear that if you do meet a potential marriage partner, life is great, exciting, the future full of promise. And if you don't meet one, life is still great, exciting, the future full of promise. You can't lose either way.

Now having attained this level of awareness and acceptance about yourself, you are indeed ready for a trip to the altar. But until that potential mate appears, if ever, how do you live a life of singleness?

Starting with your attitude, the attitude of acceptance and forgiveness, you can admit, "I am single and may very well remain single for the rest of my life, and if that happens, it is okay with me." Go back and read, in chapter three, the testimonies of CK, YEC, and WB and LJ if you haven't already. It was their unwavering trust in God despite the schemes of Satan, the enticements of the world, and the lure of the flesh that enabled them to experience periods of perfect peace during their time of singleness.

The development of trust in God and His Word is foremost a decision of the will, followed by a lifetime of meditation and study in the Bible to test and affirm the claims of God, as well as to learn of His defining attributes, especially of His love for us. Yet we need to do more than just *knowing about* God. We need to be able to say that we *know* God. There is a significant difference between these two statements.

Do not succumb to emotions as inspired by Satan, the world, and the flesh to cause you to waver in your trust. Hannah Whitall Smith in her book, *The Christian's Secret to a Happy Life*, likened emotions to the caboose of a freight train and the will to the train's engine, (see Figure 2, The Engine and the Caboose). Do not let the caboose pull the train! Talk to yourself out loud (the will), and do not listen to your self (the emotions)! David in Psalm 42:11 and Psalm 43:5 (NIV) made the very same plea.

Do not become discouraged when you are assailed by doubts. This is common to all Christians, especially to those new in the faith. Continue reading and meditating daily from your bible. Psalm 119 (NIV) is a powerful antidote to ward off the blues. So is prayer. Praying back to God in the form of praise from what you have just read is also a powerful deterrent. You will discover, over time, that your faith and trust are becoming stronger.

FIGURE 2 | THE ENGINE & THE CABOOSE

Do not let the emotions pull the engine.
Review Decision Making Process on page 93

Prayer
Bible
Counselors
Holy Spirit
Providence
Prayer

Emotions   Will

Continue building your trust by finding, if you haven't already, a Bible-believing church. You will recognize such a church by its members, who for the most part are carrying Bibles. Other qualities to look for are friendliness, warmth, a sense of joy and excitement. Did someone from the staff contact you after your first visit to welcome you and offer advice on what Sunday school class to attend?

One that would be age appropriate and provide fellowship? Join the church's singles' Sunday school class or one wherein you feel welcome and comfortable. Participate in church activities, join the choir, attend a midweek Bible study, be available to be of service to someone who has a need, and be faithful in your tithing. Above all, continue in your daily practice of prayer (out loud, when possible) and Bible study.

Charles H. Spurgeon, a nineteenth century pastor and author, recommended "hiding the Word in your heart," i.e., memorization. He was especially emphatic on committing Psalm 119 to memory. Read it and see if you agree.

As you experience life, you will no doubt find, and memorize, verses of comfort and encouragement that were particular to your circumstances at the time. Put these verses to memory also. You will never forget them because you have experienced them personally. You may also, no, you *will* have an opportunity to share them with someone who has a need to hear and apply these particular verses in their own walk.

Ask the senior pastor or someone else that you respect to provide the names of two or three older godly people, any one of whom could act as a mentor, someone that you could share with in confidence, someone that you could use as a sounding board.

Over the years my wife, Lynn, has been blessed by having the opportunity to be available to many younger women. They look upon her as an older sister and, in some cases, as a mother. In fact, they share with her things they wouldn't even tell their own mothers. Many of these relationships have continued over the years to this very day. (Relax, ladies, she doesn't relay your secrets to me, either.) In time you, too, *will* have the opportunity to be a mentor.

Some men are reluctant to share their thoughts with another man, especially if he is an older man. It's a "macho" thing or, better yet, call it like it is, "pride." Don't let pride stand in the way of receiving sage advice and counsel. Many a deep and long-time friendship has been formed through a mentoring relationship, to the benefit of both participants.

Be circumspect in your relationships with the opposite sex. Restrict your dating to group activities, and if you meet someone that is of interest, find out first if they are a believer. Do not date an unbeliever. Why? For four reasons. One, remember the triangle from the previous chapter? You will be unequally yoked (II Corinthians 6:14, "do not be unequally yoked with an unbeliever") and the chances for a long-standing serious relationship leading to a successful marriage are slim. Better to break the relationship up before it becomes serious.

Secondly, like the lyrics from an old song, to paraphrase: "breaking up is hard to do..." Don't set yourself up for another case of heartache, and if you care at all for this person, even if just a little, don't give them the hope that you have a future together. Spare them that pain of separation also. Do it early in the relationship, or better yet, as soon as you determine their relationship with God. Spare the two of you from the anguish of a breakup after a long relationship.

A testimony: GJ (Maryland) was a young man home for the summer from college. At the time, he was dating a young lady from his high school class. When asked by his father if she was a believer, his reply was "no."

"Well," said his father, "What would God have you do?"

As much as it pained GJ to do so, he ended the relationship. Two weeks later, while working a summer job as a security guard in a department store, he met a young lady who was also working a summer job at the same store as a salesperson behind the jewelry counter (how convenient). According to GJ, she met all the requirements for a godly wife. Two years later after graduation from college, they were married. Now after twenty-seven years and three sons, they still marvel and laugh whenever they hear the song, "I Met a Million Dollar Baby in a Five and Ten Cent Store." GJ's obedience was rewarded with a successful marriage.

Thirdly, do not think that you alone can bring an unbeliever to the Lord. That is the responsibility of the Holy Spirit. So getting married in the hope that later on they will become a believer through your efforts will, in all likelihood, end in failure. Ask yourself, now be honest just like GJ, is marrying an unbeliever being obedient?

Fourthly, if a relationship is on its way to becoming more than a friendship, remain chaste. Do not confuse lust for love. If someone is truly in love, they will not be turned away by a refusal to have sex before marriage. Do not fall prey to the lie, "Let's move in together and see if we are compatible." Too many hearts have been broken when the deceiver tires of the chase and departs. Unfortunately, Hollywood doesn't depict that view, only the view that it is okay, fun, glamorous, and besides, everybody is doing it. Better to be sad for a day than miserable for a lifetime. So stay chaste, save yourself for the marriage bed, and keep clear of the worldview. The nonbeliever will follow the pack, "if it feels good" do it. This is how animals act. As a believer you have committed yourself to be accountable to God and not to succumb to the world view.

Take time now, in your single life of acceptance, to give attention to your health and fitness. Start with a medical checkup. Your doctor will also have available pamphlets dealing with nutrition and exercise. Join a health club. Run and/or walk three miles a day at least three times a week, preferably five times. Don't walk alone for two reasons! One, for companionship and two, for safety. There are just too many predators lurking in the bushes.

In my view, one of the most complete books on health, exercise, and diet (it even contains recipes) is one entitled *Slimmer, Younger, Stronger* by Sam Varner, CSCS.

Varner was a conditioning coach for the New York Giants, the Clemson University football team when they were the National Champions, as well as for the 1981-1982 US Olympic Ski Team. You will benefit from Varner's coaching as did the athletes under his tutelage.

Having just completed this chapter, are you beginning to feel a sense of accomplishment and well being? A sense that everything is going to get better? If so you are making progress! If you feel that progress is not being made, I would suggest you talk with a pastor/counselor to help you get on track. Perhaps you could review the foregoing with him. He may also have other material for you to study.

VICTORY AS A
SINGLE WITH CHILDREN

I f you skipped over the previous section (Victory as a Single) because you have children, go back immediately and read it. Everything that was in this section for the single person is still applicable to the parent with one or more children, whether or not the children are at home full-time, half-time, every other weekend, or whenever. The goal, remember, is to reach the state of forgiveness and continue maturing to the "point of acceptance." You cannot force the children to do the same, but you can influence them to follow your lead, by your demeanor, to the goal of forgiveness.

The sharing of children between two households is a complex problem. To make the situation work and to be as successful as possible for all, especially for the children, ground rules and priorities must be established, agreed upon by both parents, and adhered to. This is important. The sharing or withholding of children must never be used as a bargaining chip or as an opportunity to get even with the other parent for whatever happened to have caused the divorce. The children are the innocent parties! Remember that in most cases, they love both parents, although right now, they may be angry with one or both. So please, do not use them as tools to exact revenge. If you have done this or are doing it, what is the necessary step to reach the "goal" (point of acceptance) besides stop doing it? It's *forgiveness!* Ask for forgiveness from your former spouse and your children, but only if the children are mature enough to understand. I know that someone will say to that: "My ex isn't mature enough, either." But that's okay! In their case, reciprocation, while nice to receive, is not necessary for your peace of mind. It is for theirs, however.

The time-sharing can be frustrating not only for the parents but for the children as well. In my view, the less disruption in a child's life in moving back and forth between the two households, the better off the children will be.

In the vast majority of divorces, the children will remain with their mother, and visitation rights are granted to their father.

What are your thoughts about this?

_____

_____

_____

_____

_____

_____

DISCIPLINE

Before leaving this section, the subject of discipline must be thought over and implemented. Was discipline in the home prior to the breakup nonexistent, lax (hit and miss), or too strict? Whatever it was, discipline that is firm, fair, consistent, and age- and gender-appropriate must be put in place for the following reasons:

1. to maintain peace and tranquility within the home or out in public, a restaurant for example. (Be patient, this may take time, however exasperating it may be, depending on the degree of discipline that you are starting with.)

2. to demonstrate that you love your child. The Book of Proverbs has many verses dealing with discipline. One is "He who spares the rod hates his son, but he who loves him is careful to discipline him" (Proverbs 13:24, NIV). Read a chapter a day in the book of Proverbs. You will be amazed at God's wisdom, which is applicable for all situations and occasions. Even better, read a chapter after dinner with your children. There is your authority; it's in God's Word. When the children question your authority, refer them back to God: "He is the one who said it. Go tell Him your complaint. I'm just being obedient to His instructions." That always ended any further complaining in our home regarding behavior and conse-

quences. Another ploy was "None of my friends have to do this." My answer was "They don't live here. You do."

3. to develop a healthy respect for authority in the home, at school, in the workplace, for the government, and in the armed forces. Could it be that many of our country's problems of today can be traced back, in part, to a lack of applied discipline in the home? There is no doubt in my mind that that is true.

What are your thoughts on discipline?

_____

_____

_____

_____

_____

_____

FOR FATHERS

For fathers: Resist the temptation to become a "Disneyland Dad." This is a fun and games time as opposed to meaningful time spent between father and child. It's okay once in a while, but not as a steady diet for every visit. Use these times as opportunities to teach the boys how to be men, gentlemen at that, including such seemingly little things as how to shake hands. It is incredible to me how many grown men do not know how to do this. A limp hand and a look everywhere except into the eyes of the recipient doesn't meet muster. The best way for a young man to learn how to become a godly young man is to study the book of Proverbs. In addition, it is important for fathers or father figures to spend quality time each week with the son using the book of Proverbs to inculcate God's direction for manly behavior into their lives.

Our youngest daughter would always instruct any new beau at our first meeting to "look my dad in the eye when you shake his hand. And give him a firm handshake!" I shook many a clammy hand. At that point I would ask the question, "What time will you be bringing my daughter back home?" They always brought her back home at or before the time agreed upon, too. I wonder why.

Take your daughter out on a date night. Show her, by your example, what to expect and deserve in terms of respect from their date. Do such things as ring the door bell, not honk the horn and expect her to run to the car. Give her flowers and escort her to the car and open the car door for her. Escort her to the table, hold her chair as she sits, place her selection for dinner with the waiter. Enjoy the dinner with fun and good conversation. Just curious, but did you ever act this way with your wife before the divorce? Or did your husband?

Show interest in their schoolwork and activities. Attend as a spectator or as an adult leader in sporting or other events, even if it means sacrificing some of your time. You will find that it isn't a sacrifice. Indeed the bond between you and your child will grow in strength.

Above all, treat your sons with love and respect as a father, not as a buddy. The vast majority of men that I have counseled over the years had no relationship with their father, or it was strained at best. You have to earn their love and respect just as you have to do with your daughter(s). Use God the Father as your example; be firm, fair, and consistent in your relationship with your children. You are their role model. For the boys, show them how to act as a husband and father; for the girls, show them by example what to expect from a husband and father of her children.

The foregoing is in no way meant to be your complete guide to fatherhood. But don't be dismayed, you have two sources of guidance available to you. The first is the Word of God, and the second is the counsel and guidance from the Holy Spirit. Go to the book of Proverbs, one of the five books of wisdom, and learn what you need to know as a father as well as a man, an employee or employer, and yes, even as a husband. The Holy Spirit's responsibility is to guide you into all truth so that you will be able to apply God's Word correctly and in love. The Holy Spirit is just one of the benefits of being a child of God and a follower of Jesus Christ. If you haven't declared yourself for Christ or are still undecided, go back and re-read Part Two. Now, what would you add to this section?

_____

_____

_____

_____

_____

_____

FOR MOTHERS

For mothers: If necessary, buy a book on etiquette. Teach yourself and your children by your example. You won't regret it and neither will they when, later on, they get into situations such as "Which fork do I use at the dinner table" or "How do I set a table?" Save them from embarrassment when they get into company they wish to impress or even if it is just with plain folks, they too deserve no less than polite behavior (and that also means hats off at the dinner table!).

Teach them to say, "Yes, sir" or "Yes, ma'am." One of the many things we love and enjoy about the South is the politeness of most of the younger set. For example, the way they address older folks; it's "Mr. Bill" or "Miss Lynn," as the case may be, not being too formal yet not being impertinent or bold either. We love it, although I have to admit that I really must look old; it seems that just about every one now calls me Mr. Bill.

Much of what was written for the fathers above is also applicable to the mothers, especially as a role model for the boys in what to expect in a wife and mother of their children. As for the girls, teach them how to be godly wives for their future husbands as well as mothers for their children. This would include teaching the girls how to keep their rooms cleans (as well as the boys), to do their laundry, manage their allowances and instill an interest in preparing meals and setting the table. The best way for a young man or young woman to learn how to become a godly young person is to study the book of Proverbs. Also important is honest discussion about sex and what to expect physically as they go through puberty. Mothers also need to discuss with both her sons and daughters how to treat the opposite sex with respect within biblical guidelines.

In all likelihood, the children will be spending the majority of time with you in your home. Set the ground rules for their behavior and the consequences for misbehavior.

Communicate these rules to their father. As much as it may pain you to do so, ask if he has any suggestions. Incorporate them, if appropriate, into the rules. Both of you are to remember that this is for the children's sake and betterment, and not a contest of wills between the two of you. Try to reach agreement that these rules will also be enforced at his house when the children are on his turf. As noted before, be firm, fair, and consistent in applying these rules.

In all probability, as a divorced mother, you may have to work. The children could become "latchkey kids." If at all possible, arrange your work schedule so that you are there when they leave for school and back just before they come home from school. It is not an impossible situation. Part-time work, although it would provide a lower income and a possible loss of benefits, would preclude paying out sitters' fees. But most importantly, you will be there when the child comes home upset and crying for whatever reason.

As a single mom, this kind of situation can become a reason to marry again: "I can't do it alone," etc. But as was presented in Part One, this is a wrong reason to marry. Reread the testimonies in Part Two and remember, while perhaps you believe that you can't do it just by yourself, you are not alone. You have the power of the Holy Spirit available to you, the same power that raised Jesus from the grave, as well as comforting and reassuring verses from Scripture that have come from God, Himself, through the prophets. Verses such as "Trust in the LORD with all your heart and lean not on your own understanding" (Proverbs 3:5, NIV); and "I can do everything through Him who gives me strength" (Philippians 4:13, NIV). Spend time in prayer and meditating on the words and promises of Christ. Share your concerns with other believers, people that you trust, your pastor and the older woman mentor. Have them all join you in prayer. If you have found a Bible-believing church, as was described above, you may find certain church members will be able to provide practical assistance, like free babysitting or church programs appropriate to your needs and interests. For example these could be exercise classes, mom and daughter retreats, etc.

Remember, your goal is to reach beyond forgiveness to the "point of acceptance" as you grow in your relationship with Christ. Expect Him to help you (that's called trust), and He will.

FOR BOTH FATHERS AND MOTHERS

For both fathers and mothers: you will be challenged in many ways, of that you can be assured. Here are two lists to help you navigate these troubled waters, entitled respectively, the "Do" and the "Don't" lists.

THE DO LIST

Do act with civility toward your former spouse, especially in the presence of your children.

Do keep your promises and commitments for picking up or delivering the children as agreed upon with your ex-spouse.

Do be on time with child support and/or alimony payments.

Do be prepared to answer tough questions, such as "Why did you leave Dad (or Mom)?" Sometimes the appropriate answer is, "You will have to ask your father (or mother) that question." In any case, tell the truth as simply as you can without adding extraneous details, perhaps as an attempt to justify your own actions. Usually that one answer satisfies their curiosity, at least for now. Some will never ask. It is an issue too hurtful for them to even think about, much less discuss. The answer? Show love by giving affection and sharing quality time with them on a one-on-one basis.

Do expect to see changes in behavior. This is a time when you will have to put aside your own grief and anger and attend to your children's needs. They need to feel loved and have to be assured that nothing they did caused the breakup of the family.

Do spend time, individually, with each of your children. Remember and follow through on any promises you make. Don't leave your child waiting by the telephone or mailbox for your promised call or letter that never comes. You will pay a price for your forgetfulness, if not now, then later, when perhaps it will be too late.

Do, with your children's participation, prepare a list of chores, i.e., who will do what and when, as well as the consequences for failure to perform. Ask them to suggest what the consequences should be for each infraction. You will be amazed to find that in most instances, their penalties will be far more severe than what you would have decreed. With their help also, determine the priorities of action. For example, in order of priority: chores, homework, then free time.

Promptness and punctuality need to be understood and adhered to. Ask them what time they expect to be home from an outing with their friends (the time has to fall within a period that you feel is acceptable). However tacky or tight they may feel, it is when you penalize them for being even just one minute late that you are preparing them to live and work in a world that demands punctuality, not only in business but as a courtesy to others. Besides, it will keep you from worrying yourself to death if they are late, which brings to mind that a call is expected if the deadline will be exceeded. You will hear some of the most outrageous and bizarre excuses for lateness ever coined. Remember them because some time later, much later, you and your children will enjoy a good laugh over their ingenuity at tall tale telling. Nevertheless, a time of "grounding" should be assessed for each infraction. The penalty should have been agreed upon with their participation, along with the other rules of conduct and consequences.

Do have fun as a family. You, as the parent, need to set the tone of the home. Be cheerful, see the glass half full, not half empty. Plan fun things to do in the home and on outings.

Do show love and affection for each member of the family. Encourage them, by your example, to love one another. This is the most important "Do" on the list.

Jesus said that the second greatest commandment was to love others as yourself, the first being to "Love the Lord your God with all your heart and with all your soul and with all your mind" (Matthew 22:37, NIV).

What "Do" would you add?

_____

_____

_____

_____

_____

_____

THE DON'T LIST

Do not "bad-mouth the other parent." After all, the children love them even if you no longer do.

Do not ask the children to carry messages, verbally or otherwise, to the other party. Keep them out of it. Send the message by mail, telephone, or e-mail, or whatever else is new these days, without compromising privacy.

Do not ask the children what is going on at the other house. Chances are the children will reveal it in general conversation anyway. If you need to know, trust that God will reveal it to you. He will.

Do not have your "friend" stay the night with you while the children are visiting. When the time comes that marriage is in the offing, then that will be the time enough to do the introductions, as there may be many candidates in between. Instead, be a good example to your children by restraining yourself till the marriage bed.

Do not let the children play you one against another. This is one of the reasons why it is important to keep the communication open, and at a civil level, between the two of you. One of the children may ask or even demand to go live with the other parent. Why is this request being asked? Is it for legitimate reasons or a ploy to gain an advantage? You and the ex need to be in agreement, and the child also needs to know that if this request is granted, there is no return ticket. It is a one-way trip.

Add any "Don't" that you feel is important.

_____

_____

_____

_____

_____

_____

TIME FOR REFLECTION AND ENCOURAGEMENT

Whatever stage you are at, getting a divorce, divorced, in recovery, or singleness with or without children, this book has been made available to you. Does this chapter, especially the part dealing with a single parent with children, strike a spark of fear and anxiety in you? Does it raise a question of anguish and self-doubt? "Can I manage all this by myself?" or, "What are we doing to ourselves and the children?" or, in the past tense, "What have we done?" The emotions are at work. Do not let the caboose pull the train, remember?

Ask yourself this question: Is a reconciliation possible? As long as a third party is present, reconciliation is not possible. Nor is it wise to even consider reconciliation if the departed spouse is still walking in darkness. But shouldn't we try to stay together for the children's sake? That is a choice only the two of you can make. It will require the services of a skilled pastoral counselor who, with the help of the Holy Spirit and the Word of God, can help facilitate changed behavior and thought patterns. After all, the two of you did at one time vow to love one other "till death do you part." Is it possible to restore that love? With God anything is possible. Jesus, when asked by the disciples how many times do we forgive, replied, "seventy times seven." A legal separation may be an option while the two of you are working on a restoration with the help of that skilled pastoral counselor mentioned above.

Do not become like the mother of eight, desperate for security, who gave herself to almost every man that came along in the hope of gaining a husband. In my experience, there are very few men, if any, who would be willing to marry and take on eight step-children in a trade for sexual favors, no matter how sensuous and delightful these favors may be.

Instead, keep your eye on Jesus. Gather your prayer warriors about you and go to Him who comforts and reassures. Recall such verses as "Cast your cares on the Lord and He will sustain you; He will never let the righteous fall" (Psalm 55:22, NIV). Tell Him your concerns, and "cast your cares" at the foot of the cross. Claim the promise in Isaiah 26:3: "You will keep in perfect peace him whose mind is steadfast because he trusts in You," and do what the verse says to do, keep focused on all the attributes and promises of Jesus. That is your job. His job is to give you perfect peace. He will. It's a promise. The more you do your part, the more you will see Him doing His. Expect it.

In the meantime, do not neglect yourself. Join in group activities such as exercise programs, theater, outdoor and indoor activities with other single parents and their children, and develop same-sex friendships (you read it right, same-sex friends). Go back and re-read the testimonies in Part Two and rejoice in their victories, which can be yours, too.

In what other ways can you apply yourself to reach the goal of "I am happy single or married (the point of acceptance)"? I can't lose either way because I have committed my life to the Lord's will.

_____

_____

_____

_____

_____

_____

PART FOUR:

THE COURTSHIP

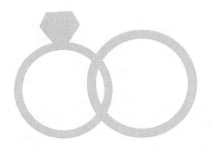

COURTSHIP AS A SINGLE WITH OR WITHOUT CHILDREN

Having attained this level of awareness about yourself, the point of acceptance, you are ready for a second marriage should that opportunity present itself. So if someone comes along that you feel attracted to, be cautious. Do they know Jesus as Savior? If not, do not proceed any further with the relationship. As said before in GJ's testimony, better to end the relationship now before a strong emotional bond develops. Why is this so important? The last thing either one of you want to have happen is to enter into a relationship that ends, once again, in the tragedy of divorce. Almost all, if not all, men and women have the same fear of failure in a second attempt at marriage. The old adage, "Once bitten, twice shy," applies. Being unequally yoked, a Christian married to an unbeliever, will seriously increase the chances for a failed second marriage.

How can you be sure that this will be a good match, a match that will bring fulfillment and enrichment to both husband and wife "till death due us part?" You can't! I'm sorry, but you just can't be certain. But don't despair, there is one step that each may take to ensure an almost 100 percent guarantee of a successful marriage, and that is to bring into the relationship a third party. A third party? "Are you serious?" you ask. "Who is that third party?" Ecclesiastes 4:9-12 (NIV) makes it very clear that a three-fold cord is not easily broken. Who is that third cord? It is Jesus Christ in the person of the Holy Spirit. Go back to Part Two and review Figure 1. If you haven't accepted Christ as your Savior, do so now. Who is the first priority of the couple? It is not each other, it is Jesus, with the second priority being the other person, and the self last.

Do not be misled by statistics, even by Christian statisticians, that indicate Christian marriages have the same divorce rate, fifty percent, as do secular marriages. It all depends on the definition of a Christian. Paul Little in his book, *How To Give Away Your Faith*, defined three different sorts of Christian faith: (1) indoctrination faith, no commitment to Christ but going through all the right motions; (2) conformity faith, no commitment to Christ but due to strong Christian surroundings also give the right impression (these are the ones that will most likely fall away when they go away to college); and (3) commitment faith, genuine followers of Jesus Christ.

It is my opinion, based on my experience as a counselor and pastor, that less than ten percent of the "church" people I have counseled fall into category three, a committed Christian. Of the people attending our eight-to-ten-week premarital course led by my wife and me, forty percent either decided not to get married or their post-poned wedding. To my knowledge of the sixty percent that did get married, only one couple has since divorced. I often wonder if the forty percent that decided not to get married were spared from going through the agony of a subsequent divorce?

So much for statistics. The divorce rate for those with commitment faith from the foregoing numbers, by my less than scientific calculations, is less than five percent. Want to ensure a lasting marriage? You tried marriage without God in the loop, and it didn't work. Now try it with Him. Go back to Part Two and surrender to the Lordship of Jesus if you haven't already, and learn how to be a committed Christian. The old hymn that proclaims "Victory in Jesus" is true.

The basic and fundamental requirement has now been established. The prospective partner must be a committed Christian. How is this to be determined? How do we differentiate between the "indoctrination and the conformity faiths" from the "commitment faith"? It will take time, and even then, we can't be 100 percent certain. One couple I know tested well, related well, and gave every outward appearance of being a godly pair well-suited to each other. They had even signed a covenant pledge that divorce was not an option. They had also declined to put into place a prenuptial agreement. Yet one year into the marriage, one partner dumbfounded the other by filing for a divorce. So it can happen, sad to say.

Nevertheless, start off slow in your new relationship by participating in group activities to begin with and when you are comfortable, double or triple dating with each other's friends. As the relationship progresses to just the two of you, remain chaste and keep out of each other's bedrooms. It is worth repeating again: do not confuse lust with love. No matter what Hollywood or TV depicts as fun and, besides, everyone is doing it, don't fall prey to a lie. Save yourself for the marriage bed. If your partner truly loves you, they will respect your wishes. This too is a test to determine if the walk is that of a committed Christian or that of a non-believer, the so-called indoctrination or conformity Christians.

Continue your discovery about each other. An important and valuable tool to use is a genogram. Go to Google.com and type in "genogram." In my view, Wikipedia gives one of the best descriptions on how to use this great tool for pictorially showing a family tree as well as showing relationships between its members, patterns of behavior, heredity, psychological factors, and more. Go back at least two generations in each of your families. The purpose of genograms is to make it easier to understand the complexity of family history, patterns and relationships between family members. By so doing, it will be much simpler to evaluate the family's strengths and vulnerabilities. This would also reveal patterns of illnesses, divorces, marital relationships, etc. It may require separate genograms for each category.

Use the following pages to document your findings. Give full disclosure on each item. This does not mean it is necessary to give all the details. One couple, in for counseling, were at odds with each other because the husband had not told his wife about a past relationship. No name or details were necessary, just the fact that the husband had been engaged. As it turned out, the husband had not only been engaged once before, but twice. He had been afraid that if he told her, she wouldn't marry him. That rubber band of trust had now been stretched. The nagging question that remained was, "Is there anything else?" Remember, be truthful in the exercise that follows:

PARENTS: Married, divorced, deceased? Blue or white collar? Highest education level achieved? Religion? Habits, good or bad? Where did they grow up as children? How many siblings did they each have? Relationships between family members, etc.?

_____

_____

_____

_____

_____

_____

SIBLINGS: How many? Gender? Your position in the birth stream? Sibling rivalry?

Where are they now? What was your relationship to them growing up? The relationship now, etc.?

_____

_____

_____

_____

_____

_____

MARRIAGES: Once? Twice? In my experience, I have met two men who were each married seven times. Is either one a good risk for marriage? Surprisingly, one in my view is. Six years ago he surrendered his life to Jesus. He is truly a changed person (Ephesians 4:24, NIV). What else could you ask for?

_____

_____

_____

_____

DIVORCES: How many and why? Who filed? Was any attempt made to reconcile? Are you paying child support? How much and for how long? Alimony and how much? (These are need-to-know answers for developing a budget when you are married.) Anything else?

_____

_____

_____

PAST RELATIONSHIPS: Remember it is not necessary to disclose every detail. Who left whom and why would be appropriate. So would questions such as "Are you marrying me on the rebound?" or, "Are you still carrying a torch for this person?" Look each other in the eye when you ask these questions.

_____

_____

_____

_____

CHILDREN: How many? How old? Gender? Where are they now? Do you see them? How often? Child support and how much? (One young man fathered a child with a young girl. He married her. Then he fathered a child with another woman, returned home, and fathered a second child with his wife, only to leave again for a different woman. He got her pregnant, too. Unbelievably, he returned home and fathered a third child with his wife, his fifth child that we know of.) That is why questions such as these are asked. There are men in this world who have no conscience, no sense of honor and decency, and women who are foolish enough to believe the lie: "I'm sorry, but I'll change, I promise."

_____

_____

EDUCATION: Dropout? High school? College? Degree(s)? Other? How was tuition paid? By whom? Was school, no matter what level, fun?

_____

_____

_____

EMPLOYMENT HISTORY: What was your first job? What is your job now? Does this show opportunity for advancement? Who have you worked for and for how long? Why did you leave each position? Do you enjoy and are you excited about what you do?

_____

_____

_____

_____

FINANCIAL HISTORY: Have you ever declared bankruptcy? Do you have credit card debt? How much? Have you ever made a balance sheet? If so, what is your net worth? Do you operate on a budget? (Sad to say, some second marriages start off with each of the couples maintaining separate cash and checking accounts and paying

their own bills. It doesn't work like that. More later.)
What more would you like to know?

_____

_____

_____

_____

MILITARY SERVICE: What branch of the service? How
long? What did you do? Receive any decorations? What
rank did you attain? What kind of discharge, etc.?

_____

_____

_____

_____

CRIMINAL RECORD: If so, what? Full details required.
Any DUI's or other infractions?

_____

_____

_____

HEALTH: Have you ever had or have now a STD (sexu-
ally transmitted disease)?
    When did you last have a full physical? What were
the results? Have you had cancer? Is it in remission?

_____

_____

_____

_____

ADDICTIONS: This does not necessarily apply to physical addictions, such as drugs and alcohol, but also to gambling, TV, pornography, work, to anything that is a higher priority than spouse and family. Any one of these can be the cause of a marital break-up and unhappiness for the entire family.

_____

_____

_____

HOBBIES: What are your hobbies? Are they expensive and time-consuming? Can they be shared with spouse and family?

_____

_____

_____

_____

OUTDOOR ACTIVITIES: Do you participate in activities such as camping, hiking, tennis, golf, boating, swimming, fishing, bowling, softball, etc.?

_____

_____

_____

_____

OTHER: What would you like to add?

_____

_____

_____

Another viable tool is a "time line" sketch for each of your lives. Go to Figure 3, page 90. The left end of the time line is labeled "Birth." At the right end, it is labeled the "Present." In between these two points show all the significant events that have occurred in your life during this segment of time. Show the arrows up for positive events and down for negative ones. On the blank lines that follow the time line, write in the meaning and significance of each arrow. Meditate on these events. How have they influenced your present outlook on life, your character, your relationship with others, your faith, etc.? Did you learn anything new about yourself, such as patterns of behavior? Did you have any "Aha!" moments? If so, what did you discover? Use the blank lines on page 91 for your answers.

FIGURE 3 | TIME LINE (EXAMPLE)

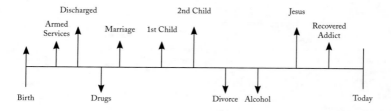

Make several time lines on a separate sheet of paper:

One for Career

One for Family Life

One for Other?

_____

_____

_____

_____

_____

_____

_____

_____

_____

_____

_____

_____

_____

_____

_____

_____

_____

_____

_____

_____

_____

_____

_____

_____

The foregoing are exercises in communication. You are sharing yourself, even to the point of vulnerability, to the other person. You are building trust and intimacy, a strong start for a future relationship.

A TIME FOR REFLECTION

If you have gotten this far in your discovery about each other and you are still together, hooray! And if you have parted ways, hopefully as friends, it's still hooray!

One true sign of maturity is the ability to not only discern the truth, but be able to communicate that truth, in love, to the other party. Don't allow yourself to be dragged along in a halfhearted relationship because you don't want to hurt the other person's feelings by ending it. If you have any doubts or questions, they should be asked now. To continue the relationship is not only unfair to the other person but to yourself as well. It takes courage to speak up. But it must be done. Marriage demands a full commitment of mind, body, and spirit. To do anything less is, in my view, a betrayal and a lack of integrity by the one who fails to speak up. And if it is the other party who wishes to break off the relationship, accept it graciously. However, you are entitled to know why. Consider it a learning experience, a time of growth, and give praise. This is why courtship was invented, to learn about one another; are we compatible or not? There are six, no, seven steps to further assist in making the second most important decision you will ever make.

BIBLICAL DECISION-MAKING

1. Putting your faith and trust in Jesus as your Savior.
2. Prayer. Ask for wisdom in making a decision that will be in accordance with the will of God (James 1:5, NIV).
3. The Bible. What does the Word of God say about second marriages?
4. Counselors. There is wisdom in many a counselor (Proverbs 12:15, NIV).
5. Providential Circumstances (Romans 8:28, NIV).
6. Holy Spirit. He will guide us into all truth... (John 16:13, NIV).
7. More prayer. Ask for the peace that comes with knowing that the two of you are doing God's will for your lives.

After completing the foregoing exercises, and if each of you are satisfied and at peace with the answers given, the relationship has become serious. It is now time to plan on how the two of you will make the transition into a one-family household with or without children. Planning the wedding itself comes after the transition plans are completed.

FOR SINGLES WITH CHILDREN

For those with children, it is now time to introduce your friend to your children as well as being introduced to your friend's children, if you haven't already. A caution here: do not introduce each other as their future parent, especially if you have been parading a series of prospective parents for their review and comment. (That could become a joke between the children: "Here is Dad's [or Mom's] parent of the month.") In truth, the decision to marry is not theirs to make, it is yours. Certainly you want their input, which will need to be evaluated by both you and their future parent. Be prepared for some negative reaction at this first meeting from either one or both sets of children, especially if the divorce has been fairly recent. (A caution here, review the statistics in Part One on marrying too soon.) They may very well view each of you as interlopers taking the place of their respective, departed parent. They may also be planning, or are hopeful at least, that their parents may reconcile. Your appearance here could, in their mind, preclude that from ever happening. So be prepared, and above all, be authentic. Children can sense when they are being patronized, even if they aren't old enough to know what that word means.

Now with these cautions set forth, you may have some of your own. If so, what are they?

_____

_____

Have fun at these times together. Do what families normally do for recreation. Once a relationship has been established between each of the prospective stepparents and the prospective stepchildren, it is time to bring the two families together. It will soon be obvious to each set of children that this will likely become their new family. Write down your thoughts and observations on how well the first and subsequent meetings went with the combined children. Use the following space to list both positive and negative concerns either one or both of you have observed.

Remember, the decision to move forward with the relationship is your decision, not the children's. But you would be wise to get their buy-in by being authentic.

You have now gathered enough information, observed relationships between future spouse and children and between children of both families. It is now time to commit this to prayer.

PART FIVE:

IS THIS THE ONE FOR ME?

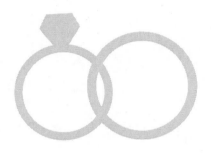

PREMARITAL COUNSELING: WITH OR WITHOUT CHILDREN

I f you have applied yourself in using the previous four Parts to get this far, you are ready to begin premarital counseling. This means that you understand what went wrong in the first marriage, have given forgiveness, understand the need for the third party (Jesus) in a marriage, reached the "point of acceptance," and now have met what appears to be a suitable life partner. As you continue to learn more about each other and how to react in a godly way under various trials, the two of you will draw closer and accept each other. Read aloud, together, from the King James Version "The Song of Solomon," chapter 2, verses 10-13:

> My beloved spake, and said unto me, Rise up, my love, my fair one, and come away. For, lo, the winter is past, the rain is over and gone; The flowers appear on the earth; the time of the singing birds is come, and the voice of the turtle is heard in our land. The fig tree putteth forth her green figs, and the vines with the tender grape give a good smell. Arise my love, my fair one, and come away.

This is love as God intended, between a man and a woman, sweet and pure. The two of you are in love. Enjoy these moments of discovery. The honeymoon will be even better. God has a sense of humor. He even tells us what side of the bed to sleep on (Song of Solomon 2:6, NIV).

What is love? The Bible defines love in four ways: agape (a sacrificial love that is unconditional); phileo (a brotherly love, both words are in the New Testament); storge (a love between family members, Old Testament only), and eros (sexual love). Read 1 Corinthians 13, and list the various definitions of love.

_____

_____

_____

_____

_____

_____

_____

_____

The premarital counseling starts with a personality evaluation test of yourself and your future partner. There are several personality tests available to help the two of you make a wise and informed decision on a second marriage. One is the Taylor-Johnson Temperament Analysis

(1-800-345-8378) by Psychological Publications, Inc. Another is the Carlson Learning Company's DiSC-Personal Profile System, (1-847-259-0005). For more information on these companies and their programs, go to Google.com or call the telephone numbers enclosed in the parentheses. Another program, one that I highly recommend, is the Prepare/Enrich program by Life Innovations, Inc. Their Web site is: www.lifeinnovations. com.

Your pastor or your counselor should be able to administer and review the test results with you. Did you take any one of these tests, or one similar, before your first marriage? If you did, was your profile different this second time? How?

_____

_____

_____

Premarital is synonymous with preplanning. Where will we live? What rules do we follow? Who does what, etc.? Most of these questions will be answered, if not all, by examining what is involved in each of the following nine general areas of married life: (1) Spirituality; (2) Communication; (3) Finance; (4) Health; (5) Sex; (6) Recreation; (7) Children (will be discussed in much greater detail in the next section); (8) Planning for the future; and (9) Miscellaneous.

SPIRITUAL

The Bible, in Ephesians 5:22-38 (NIV), defines the relationship between husband and wife and their relationship with God. The Bible commands us not to be unequally yoked with unbelievers, (2 Corinthians 6:14, NIV). See Figure 4, which is shown here again for ease in reviewing and discussing.

In my view, there is no better way to portray the power that is available to a couple in a Christian marriage than that which is depicted in Figure 4. Christ, in the person of the Holy Spirit, indwells both believers, joining all three together under God the Father's umbrella of protection.

Each has direct access to God through Jesus (John 14:6, NIV). The Holy Spirit prays for us, provides comfort and, among other attributes, interprets scripture for our understanding and promotes unity in decision-making. Think of the power available to bring about that unity in decision-making. This is one of the reasons not to be unequally yoked to an unbeliever.

The Bible in Romans 8:29 (NIV) tells us to become conformed to the image of Christ. This is called sanctification. Notice in Figure 4 that the closer the husband and wife draw to Jesus the closer they draw to each other.

FIGURE 4 | EQUALLY YOKED

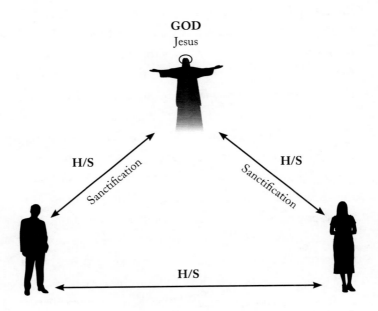

- H&W joined together by the H/S (equally yoked)
- H/S joins H&W to Jesus (God)
- H&W each have equal status with Jesus
- Overseeing the relationship is God the Father. Picture that as an umbrella of protection covering the triangular relationship.
- The closer H&W draw to Christ (through progressive sanctification) the closer they grow to one another.

This is the most important relationship in a marriage: the relationship to God through His Son, Jesus Christ. Ecclesiastes 4:9-12 makes it very clear that a threefold cord is not easily broken. Who is that cord? It is Christ in the person of the Holy Spirit. This is the power that enables couples to love one another unconditionally, to love each other as best friends and to enjoy the gift of sexual love as they truly become one flesh. This is the power to ward off the schemes of Satan. This is the power to reject the lure of the world. This is the power to reject the attractions of the flesh and to walk in the Spirit. This is the power to live a life that has meaning and one that bears spiritual fruit. And finally, this is the power that is the foundation for a successful marriage. What better way to bring honor and glory to God the Father?

It is the responsibility of the husband, as the spiritual leader, to see that the couple prays, reads, and studies scripture together. Sad to say, I have found that many men shirk or, most likely, are not aware that this is their responsibility. But here is the glory that is in the power of the Holy Spirit. Wife, there is no need to nag; ask God through the Holy Spirit to change and enable your husband to take on these duties. After all, the same Holy Spirit resides in both of you. Will this prayer bring honor and glory to God? Absolutely! God will answer, in His perfect timing, any prayer that is prayed in the name of Jesus for God's glory and in God's will. How do you determine His will? Start with prayer by asking for wisdom. Read God's Word for His answer.

PRIORITIES

The priorities, based on scripture, in a Christian marriage are as follows: God, spouse, children, work, ministry and, finally, self. See the book of Ephesians, chapters 5 and 6 (NIV). From these scripture references and others that you will find in the concordance of your bible, list the responsibilities of both husband and wife in a marriage relationship. There are many scriptures that refer to the responsibilities of both the husband and wife in the marriage relationship. They are encapsulated in Ephesians 5: 21-33 (NIV) wherein are listed the duties and obligations of marriage by each spouse. Another scripture describes the virtuous wife and that can be found Proverb 31: 10-31 (NIV).

Individually, each partner should spend time daily in prayer and study in the Bible. There should also be a time for the couple to pray, study, and discuss scripture together, whether it be in the Bible, a commentary, or a Bible study lesson. How often? Well, how often did Jesus pray and for how long? Can we use Him as an example? What will the two of you do? Be realistic.

_____

_____

_____

For those with children, God holds the parents responsible for teaching them the Word of God. After they leave home, He holds the children responsible for following and obeying the Word. More will be said about this in the following section, "Blending a Family."

When couples came to me for marriage counseling, I would ask certain questions of the husband such as "How often do you pray together?" or "How often do you study the bible together?" Now, the wife is sitting right there. The husband has no choice but to tell the truth or prove himself a liar in front of his wife. The lack of a positive response from him was, in my view, one of the reasons why they were in my office.

God has designed and appointed the man to be the spiritual leader of the family and the wife to be his help-mate. When these roles are fulfilled according to God's design, it is amazing how many of the points of contention just seem to melt away and become non-issues.

Look at Figure 4 again. We know that Christ is perfect, and we know that we are called to become like Him. Isn't it logical to assume that as we grow more like Him, the bond between husband and wife grows stronger as depicted on the diagram? The result being that strife between the two fades away and the love between them grows? The Holy Spirit is at work binding us together. You will also find that, at times, you are even thinking the same thoughts.

God's plan for marriage is perfect. All it requires for the participants to do is to seek God with all their heart, soul, and mind. The Holy Spirit will do the rest. Will we become like Jesus? The Bible teaches that we become like Him when He calls us home (1 Corinthians 13:12, NIV). See also I John 3:2. How does one seek God with all their heart, soul, and mind?

The answer to this question is the foundation of marriage and of a life worth living. Spend time on it. In fact, you will spend a lifetime answering it as you grow in Christ. Study the words of Christ in your Bible, they are often printed in red, especially the "Sermon on the Mount" (Matthew chapters 5, 6 and 7, NIV). So what is your answer? Check back in a year or so and answer the question again.

_____

_____

_____

_____

_____

_____

_____

_____

COMMUNICATION

Webster's New World Dictionary: Second College Edition, defines communication as the giving or exchanging of information by talk, gestures, writing, etc. It also defines communication as a close, sympathetic relationship. Both definitions, while valid, do not provide enough information on *how* to communicate between spouses. For instance, there are five levels in communicating our thoughts and needs to another person.

The first is by clichés: "How are you?" or "I'm good," etc. These are common talk with really no genuine interest in the other person's health or welfare, merely a way to say hello.

The second is by sharing facts. "It's a nice day," or "The Yankees won again last night." No opinions are offered. It is just a way to make small talk. Call it "safe talk."

The third level is offering an opinion. At this level you are opening yourself up to criticism or challenge. "I would like to spend our vacation in the mountains." "No, I want to spend it at the beach." Now that is conflict. Some people avoid conflict at all costs. They will either be stubborn and get their way, or be compliant to the other person's wishes. They never reveal themselves to the other person, and that is just not being honest. Or better yet, authentic.

The fourth level is feelings and emotions. At this level, each person feels safe to reveal how they feel. "I am very concerned over your reaction to your brother's health." "I really get upset when I see how some members of Congress put self and party over country."

The fifth level is intimacy. At this level, there are no barriers to communication. It is as if I am holding out my hands and handing to you my total self, warts and all, trusting you not to hurt me. That is intimacy and complete trust. This is the level each married couple works to achieve. How often have you reached level four or level five with another person? Explain, on the lines that follow:

_____

_____

_____

Before moving on to listening skills and conflict resolution, in level three above, there is another vital means of communication that needs to be entered into, and that is prayer; prayer not only by each spouse individually but collectively with God the Father. Jesus is our model. In the concordance of your Bible, look up the reference verses that deal with when and where He prayed, and list them below.

_____

_____

_____

_____

_____

The disciples asked Him to "teach us to pray." He responded with The Lord's Prayer (Luke 11:1-4 and Matthew 6:9-15, NIV). This prayer is a model. Take the key elements and use them to format an outline for your prayer, a prayer that is from the heart. The key elements are: adoration, confession, thanksgiving, and supplication (ACTS). Write out in the lines that follow a prayer to God the Father, using this outline as the skeleton for your prayer. Let this prayer deal with where you are in mind, body, and spirit, at this very moment. Say it out loud and mean it. God is listening.

_____

_____

_____

_____

_____

Martyn Lloyd Jones in his book, *The Sermon On the Mount: Volume Two,* Chapters 4-6, delivers an outstanding and comprehensive exposition of The Lord's Prayer or, as some call it, The Disciples' Prayer. If you have only two books in your library, this should be one of them. The other? Come on now. Do you really need to ask?

Back to level three: offering an opinion. How is conflict, inherent in that statement, handled in a way that will honor God? It starts with speaking and listening skills. What are they?

Speaking skills require the speaker to state clearly what they want and need. Listening skills require the listener to state back to the speaker what they heard the speaker say. (Too often the listener isn't really listening but is busy formulating a response to the speaker's position). The speaker and listener reverse roles. Again, the listener repeats back what they heard the other person say. The following steps and attitudes are one way to resolve conflict:

CONFLICT RESOLUTION

1. Select a place for discussion that will be free of interference, telephone, TV, etc.
2. Start with prayer from each of you, asking for wisdom and guidance from the Holy Spirit. This step will also bring about a state of calmness between the two parties.
3. State the problem, using the listening and hearing skills stated above.
4. Brainstorm for possible solutions.
5. Evaluate and rank the possible solutions.
6. Pick one and agree to try it. Set a time to meet again to review progress.
7. End in prayer.

I have found that ninety percent of the time the solution is found by breaking the problem down into its smallest elements.

Pick an issue that needs to be resolved between the two of you. Using these seven steps, do an exercise in the space that follows to resolve the issue.

_____

_____

_____

_____

_____

_____

_____

_____

_____

_____

FINANCES

The financial starting point in putting together two people with or without children into one family starts with a balance sheet from each before marriage, then combining them into one balance sheet on "day one" of the marriage. A balance sheet is a point in time that measures the assets against the liabilities. The difference between the two is called the net worth. In a healthy financial unit (the family), the net worth should be positive and growing in value as time passes. This, therefore, is a tool to be used as a warning if the net worth is negative. Debt will need to be reduced and/or assets must be increased. Managing the cash flow will solve the problem. The following exercise is a short example for calculating net worth. Google. com has many sources to obtain help in developing your net worth as well as do stationary stores and accounting firms. Computer software is also available.

BALANCE SHEET

for period ending
dd/mm/yyyy

ASSETS

Cash	$_____
Cash value of Real Estate	_____
Cash value of Stocks, Bonds, etc.	_____
Cash value of autos, boats, etc.	_____
Cash value of jewelry, furniture, etc.	_____
Cash value of all other assets	_____
Total	$_____

LIABILITIES

Total credit card debt	$_____
Mortgage(s), balances	_____
All loan balances, autos, boats, student, etc.	_____
All other debt	_____
Total of child support and alimony to be paid	_____
Total	$_____

NET WORTH

Subtract Liabilities from Assets	$_____

Your individual balance sheets should be far more detailed. Now put them together. This is the starting point for your marriage. Evaluate the result critically. Is either one of you taking on a mountain of debt from the other? Or, conversely, a mountain of "gold"? Either way, are both of you comfortable with this? This could become a "deal breaker" for some. If it is, what does that say about commitment? Priorities? What are your thoughts?

_____

_____

_____

_____

_____

This issue needs to be resolved before the marriage. Do not take the position that "we will work it out later." You won't. It will become a source of irritation and resentment that could lead to another divorce. This is why you are doing this exercise to resolve every possible issue, to the satisfaction of everyone, before marriage. While pooling (co-mingling) the assets of both parties, each with children, starting a second marriage should not be a problem where the difference between the assets of each is small. But now, in the situation posed above where one of the partners has a significant amount of assets than does the other, what is the solution? Co-mingle? Prenuptial agreement? Separate accounts? Last Will and Testament? Other? And what does the Bible say? Do

not marry an unbeliever, marriage is a covenant relationship, become one flesh, etc. Using the seven steps for
Conflict Resolution on page 112, how would the two of
you resolve this problem? It may very well be a real issue
between the two of you. If not, it still could be a reveal-
ing exercise for each participant. If need be, go back to
page 93, Biblical Decision-Making, and review the steps
for making a decision that is in keeping with the will of
God. Here, the counsel from experts in this field (legal
and accounting) should be heavily weighted, but not at
the expense of the Word of God.

RESOLVING CONFLICT

_____

_____

_____

_____

_____

_____

_____

_____

_____

_____

_____

_____

_____

_____

BIBLICAL DECISION-MAKING

_____

_____

_____

_____

_____

_____

_____

_____

_____

_____

_____

_____

The second step is to develop a monthly cash flow based on the income and expenses of both after marriage. Wikipedia is one of many sites on Google.com that provide further instruction on the use of cash flow charts. Computer software programs are also available. Use the rudimentary template that follows, as an example, to record this information. Your actual expenses will be far more detailed.

MONTHLY CASH FLOW

CASH IN
BUDGET RECEIVED/SPENT VARIANCE

Beginning cash $_____

(Cash left over from previous month)

Payroll # 1 _____

Payroll #2 _____

Other _____

Total Cash in $_____

CASH OUT

Tithe $_____

Mortgage _____

Credit Cards _____

Utilities _____

Insurance _____

Other _____

Total Cash out $_____

Net ending cash plus or minus $_____

(becomes the beginning cash for the next month)

Make a careful assessment of the results using your actual income and expenses. Will you have a positive cash flow?

If not, what will you do about it? Write your answers in the space that follows.

_____

_____

_____

_____

These two documents, the Balance Sheet and the Cash Flow, properly maintained, with the discipline to manage spending (staying within the monthly budget), will preclude many a heated discussion in the future. Decide now who will oversee the finances. However, both husband and wife need to be aware of the financial processes regardless of who is in charge. It is a team effort.

Two words of caution: (1) keep important documents in a safety deposit box and (2) have only one credit card. Make certain that it is paid off in full each month. Do not let credit card interest consume and demolish the family budget. Remember too, when planning a family budget, that there is a difference between *needs* and *greeds*. Learn to differentiate between them.

I asked our son, before he got married, to list the bare essentials he and his wife would need to start housekeeping. The list came back with such items as TV, stereo, etc. The list failed to include one essential item, which his bride-to-be was quick to point out: a bed. The other items they deleted.

HEALTH

In Part Three, the importance of health was discussed in relationship to a single life. It is even more important in a marriage relationship. A complete physical may detect a hitherto undiagnosed disease that could lead to an early death or a severely impaired life either physically, mentally, or both. If children are involved, especially young children, do the marriage plans continue?

_____

_____

_____

Perhaps one way to approach this problem is to ask the question: "Suppose, shortly after the marriage took place, an accident took the life of the person in question. What would the surviving partner do?" Does this help answer the previous question? Remember your marriage vows. Were they taken seriously or not?

_____

_____

_____

In a previous section (Part Three), emphasis was placed on eating the right kind of food and exercise. Donuts for breakfast, junk food for lunch, and leftovers for supper just won't do it. If possible, plan the meals a month in advance. My wife did, and our children always seemed to be invited out for dinner to a friend's house on the nights we had liver and onions. It would have been fun to have those parents, unbeknownst to their children, also serve liver and onions. Too late! The opportunity has passed, but maybe not for you.

Exercise. Get the children involved, too. It may be necessary to curtail social networking time on the computer in order to insure physical activity of some kind. Families can spend time together bowling, camping, hiking, horseback riding, boating, fun at the beach, fishing or just have a picnic in the park.

What other premarital concerns should you and your intended spouse address?

_____

_____

_____

_____

You and your intended have really worked diligently to identify what is needed for a successful marriage. You have also addressed each one of these. Now is the time to devote this to prayer and perhaps even fasting. And then pray again that this is God's will for your lives.

PART SIX:

MAKING TWO EQUAL ONE

BLENDING TWO FAMILIES
INTO ONE

During the early 1970's, there was a TV show entitled, *The Brady Bunch*. The story line involved a father with three sons who married a mother with three daughters. The oldest of each parent were in high school together; the middle children were in junior high, and the two youngest were in primary school. Fortunately, the parents had the foresight to hire a live-in housekeeper with the wisdom of Solomon, and they all lived together in a four-bedroom house in a middle-class suburb of Los Angeles. The show lasted about seven years, which says something about its popularity with the viewers. As with most dramas out of Hollywood, it was a far cry from the realities of life, much less the realities of the blending of a family. What are the realities? Here are just a few: Where will we live? What schools will the children go to? Will we have to change livelihoods? Will the children get along, not only with each other, but with the stepparent, too? What if they don't? Who will do the disciplining, manage the finances? What church will we go to? No doubt you will have other concerns. What are they? How will you respond?

_____

_____

_____

_____

_____

_____

_____

_____

_____

_____

Does it seem overwhelming? At times it will seem that way. It is hard work. It is time-consuming. It will be frustrating. It will be filled with tears and, yes, laughs too. One couple said, "It was like trying to herd a bunch of feral cats." Another said, "I'm glad we did it, but I would never do it again." All of those questioned agreed that it was not only a growth experience for each parent, but that overall it was an opportunity to demonstrate how the love of Jesus, and His power, (Philippines 4:13) can work in the lives of each family member to bring harmony into the family unit, all working to bring honor and glory to God the Father. That is what it is all about. That is what our individual lives are all about. That is how it works!

There is no step-by-step procedure on how to blend two families together. Why? Because the children from each family will be different in terms of number, age, sex, individual temperament, social skills, spiritual maturity, and perhaps even of color. The possibilities in this matrix seem almost endless. The realities mentioned above will seemingly expand the matrix, for some to the point of exasperation.

But everything you need to successfully blend a family together has already been given to you in the previous sections. Using the material from Part Three: Discipline, For Fathers, For Mothers, The Do List, The Don't List, and from Part Four, For Singles with Children, develop your own plan that is unique to your situation. Use the nine blank pages in the Appendix, entitled, "Our Plan," to record your thoughts. Commit it to prayer and refer to it often.

This book has been a joy to write. My prayer, as well as my wife's, is that your eyes will be opened to the truth, and that you will feel the power of His love as the two of you plan the blending of a family. May our Lord and Savior bless you and yours richly. Amen.

APPENDIX: OUR PLAN

The plan consists of nine topics, each of which has been addressed in the foregoing text. It is now time to put into your own words the Spirit-inspired plan on how to conduct and manage the affairs of your new family. Start with prayer.

SPIRITUAL

Commit your way to the Lord; trust in Him. (Psalm 37:5, NIV)

_____

_____

_____

_____

_____

_____

_____

_____

_____

_____

COMMUNICATION

Let your conversation be always full of grace, seasoned with salt, so that you may know how to answer everyone. (Colossians 4:6 NIV)

FINANCE

The plans of the diligent lead to profit as surely as haste leads to poverty. (Proverbs 21:5 NIV)

_____

_____

_____

_____

_____

_____

_____

_____

_____

_____

_____

_____

_____

_____

_____

_____

_____

_____

_____

_____

HEALTH

...you yourselves are God's temple and that God's spirit lives within you? (I Corinthians 3:16)

_____

_____

_____

_____

_____

_____

_____

_____

_____

_____

_____

_____

_____

_____

_____

_____

_____

_____

_____

_____

_____

_____

SEX

"...may you ever be captivated by her love." (Proverbs 5:19 NIV).

_____

_____

_____

_____

_____

_____

_____

_____

_____

_____

_____

_____

_____

_____

_____

_____

_____

_____

_____

_____

_____

RECREATION

There is a time for everything, and a season for every activity under heaven... (Ecclesiastes 3:1 NIV)

CHILDREN

Train up your child in the way he should go; and when he is old, he will not depart from it. (Proverbs 22:6 NIV)

_____

_____

_____

_____

_____

_____

_____

_____

_____

_____

_____

_____

_____

_____

_____

_____

_____

_____

_____

PLANNING FOR THE FUTURE

Consider the blameless, observe the upright; there is a future for the man of peace. (Psalm 37:7 NIV)

OTHER

For as the body without the spirit is dead, so faith without works is dead also. (James 2:26 NIV)

BIBLIOGRAPHY

PART ONE: RECOVERY

Bob Burns & Tom Whiteman. *The Fresh Start Divorce Recovery Workbook.* Nashville, Tennessee: Thomas Nelson, Inc. 1998.

Elisabeth Kübler-Ross. *Death and Dying.* New York: Simon and Schuster Ltd. 1969.

John W. James and Russell Friedman. *The Grief Recovery Handbook.* New York: Harper Collins Publishers. 1998.

PART TWO: GOD'S WAY

John R. W. Stott. *Basic Christianity.* Grand Rapids, Michigan: Wm. B. Erdmans Publishing Co. 1971.

Ray C. Stedman. *Authentic Christianity.* Grand Rapids, Michigan: Discovery House Publishers. 1996.

D. Martyn Lloyd-Jones, *Studies In The Sermon On The Mount.* Grand Rapids, Michigan: W. B. Erdmans Publishing Co. 1976.

*Note: I have listed these volumes in the order of the reader's level of maturity in the Christian walk.

PART THREE: VICTORY

Hannah Whitall Smith, *The Christian's Secret Of A Happy Life*. New York: Random House. 1986.

C.H. Spurgeon, *The Treasury Of David*. Byron Center, Michigan: Associated Publishers And Authors, Inc. 1970.

Sam Varner, *Slimmer, Younger, Stronger*. Boston, Massachusetts: Element Books Inc. 2000.

PART FOUR: THE COURTSHIP

Henry Cloud & John Townsend, *Boundaries In Dating*. Grand Rapids, Michigan: Zondervan. 2000.

PART FIVE: IS THIS THE ONE FOR ME?

H. Norman Wright. *Communication, Key To Your Marriage*. Ventura, California:Regal Books. 1974.

Stuart Scott. *Communication and Conflict Resolution*. Bemidji, Minnesota: Focus Publishing Inc. 2000.

Howard Dayton. *Free and Clear (God's Roadmap To Debt-free Living)*. Chicago, Illinois: Moody Press. 2006.

Monica McGoldrick, Randy Gerson, and Sylvia Shellenberger. *Genograms, Assessment and Interventions.* New York: W. W. Norton & Company. 1999.

PART SIX: MAKING TWO EQUAL ONE

Jim Smoke. *Growing In Remarriage.* Old Tappan, New Jersey: Fleming H. Revell Company. 1990.